# The Beaut Little Book of

# *New Zealand Slang*

## *Harry Orsman*
## *Des Hurley*

I'm a bit of a dag!

So am I!

REED

First published 1994 by Reed Books, a division of Reed Publishing
(NZ) Ltd, 39 Rawene Road, Birkenhead, Auckland 10. Associated
companies, branches and representatives throughout the world.

ISBN 0 7900 0365 1

# *Introduction*

Strange words are confusing enough, but when ordinary words are given strange pronunciations, the visitor is often thrown *A over K* (see following pages).

'Do not believe your airs' should be the watchword of those not familiar with the sound of the vocal Kiwi, whose pronunciation of the vowels in words like 'air', 'fare', 'mayor', may often sound like 'ear', 'fear', 'mere'; 'ult' like 'olt'; 'al' like 'el' (and vice versa); and the 'i' in 'sit' like 'sut' ('Australia 20, New Zealand sucks' is a well known Australian sporting graffito). Unstressed syllables can be very severely *dealt to*.

So don't be surprised to hear from New Zealanders:

'Bring down *ear fears*, but fly safely.'

'Loving *mare* folly.'

'The *mere* of Wellington is genderwise female.'

'The *cheer*person Rose-anne bought the meeting toward her.'

'The Minister's charm *rarely* comes across on TV.'

'The *Affluent Peer* Board' (selling apples and peerages perhaps).

'Prime Minister Muldoon's death marked the passing of an *error*.'

'Carbine was so *revaired* as to be raised almost to *colt* status' (said of a famous racehorse — from the Old West possibly).

'That'd be snow on the *Yelps*.'

'My husband won't *wear muzzles*. He likes *puppies*' (or perhaps oysters to go with his mussels and pipis)

The following advertisement is by no means *alimentary*: 'Wanted to sell: Piano: in very rough condition but suitable for Bach.' And *wheer alse* can one taste the simple but delightful ambiguity of 'The Bishop of Dunedin's crook.'

After all this, one might feel deeply for the local who thought sextuplets were well named; or the Kiwi cat (the one with no wings who never learned to spell) who ate *tasty* cheddar and waited outside a mouse-hole with 'baited' breath.

*Harry Orsman and*
*Des Hurley*

# A

**aftermatch function**
a drinking session after a sporting event

**all cock and ribs like a musterer's dog**
very skinny

**all hands and the cook**
everybody

**amber, the amber fluid**
beer

**anklebiter**
a toddler

**ante up**
come to light with, pay up

**A over K**
polite short form of *arse over kite,* head over heels.

**appetite like a fantail**
no or little appetite

**arvo**
afternoon

**away laughing**
indicating something successfully
completed: 'Hadlee gets a century
and we're away laughing.'

**away with the fairies**
fey, 'not with it'

# B

**bach or batch**
a hut or living quarters fit only
for a bachelor; a holiday cottage

**backbone of the country**
the farming community

**banjo**
a shovel; occasionally a leg of
mutton

**barbie**
a barbecue

**barrack**
to tease, to rib

**barrack for**
to support vociferously:
'Every time we barracked for our
basketball team, it won.'

**barracouta loaf**
a long, raised-crust loaf: from a
fancied resemblance to the long,
lean, rough-backed barracouta fish

**bash**
a drinking party or spree

**battler**
one who struggles against adver-
sity or has to work hard for a living

**beaut**
something or someone fine or
outstanding; often used ironically:
'He's a beaut: never pays his
share.'

**beautee**
an exclamation of delight

**beer sandwich**
beer in lieu of lunch

**beggars afloat**
fried scones

**bend the elbow**
to have a few drinks (often, more
realistically *wet the elbow*)

**berkers**
violent or crazy (from *berserk*)

**bible-basher**
a clergyman, or violently lapsed agnostic

**biddy-bid**
a burr-bearing plant (from Maori *piripiri*)

**big bickies**
big money, large sums

**big note**
to announce wealth ostentatiously, as by flashing $100 bills

**big skite**
arrant boaster

**big smoke**
the town or city

**big spit**
a muted *technicolour yawn*

**bikie**
a member of a motorbike gang

**binder**
a solid meal

**birch itch**
an allergy to native beech trees

**bitser**
a mongrel dog; a machine, etc., made of 'bits an' pieces'

**block**
a gang rape

**blowie**
a blowfly

**bludge**
to cadge

**bludger**
a cadger; one who lives off others, hence, a term of abuse: originally a *bludgeoner*, a prostitute's pimp

**blue (*noun*)**
a mistake; a fight or brawl

**blue (*verb*)**
to spend all one's money

**blue duck**
a failure

**bluey**
(formerly) a summons to court; a traffic ticket; also a swag, one's belongings rolled in a blanket

**bodgie**
a subcultural male of the 1950s

**bomb**
an aged motor vehicle

**bonzer**
outstanding, fine, beaut

**boob, boob tatt**
prison; a skin tattoo done in prison

**boobhead**
one serving a prison sentence

**boohai, the boohai**
a remote district or area, the 'sticks' or backblocks; *up the boohai*, very much awry. As the poet Edward Lear may have said:
*On the coast of Coromandel*
*where the magic pumpkins blow*
*Lived a jughead with a handle*
*of 'Bonger Boohai Joe'.*

**boomer**
something large or outstanding of its class

**boong(a)**
an offensive word for a coloured person

**booze artist**
a heavy drinker

**boozeroo**
a pub; a drinking session

**borough council**
a small *corporation*

**bot**
a germ or bug; a sickness, e.g. 'To catch the bot.'

**box of birds**
fine, happy, going well

**brewer's goitre**
a beer-gut or pot gut

**brown-eye**
the naked arse revealed as a sign
of contempt for the revealee(s)

**brummy**
shoddy: from *Brummagen*, a name
for Birmingham

**bucket-of-water wood**
any wood (e.g. native fuchsia) too
sappy to burn

**Buckley's (chance)**
no or little chance (of success)

**buggerlugs, buggylugs**
a term of endearment

**bull-artist**
a practised liar

**bulldust**
nonsense

**bull's roar**
a measure of distance,
occasionally of success or failure:
'As a cook, he didn't come within
a bull's roar of his dad.'

**bully for you!**
an ironic or derisive exclamation

**bung**
bankrupt; broken, out of order

**burgoo**
porridge

**bushwhacker**
a bushfeller

**bust one's boiler**
to exert oneself vigorously; to
collapse through over-exertion

**buster**
old-fashioned name for a country
newspaper. (See also *southerly
buster*)

**busy as a one-armed
paperhanger**
very busy (often in a haphazard
way)

# C

**captain cooker**
a wild pig

**cardie**
a cardigan

**cast**
immobilised (e.g. through drunkenness), as of a sheep unable to get to its feet

**chateau cardboard**
an up-market name for wine in a cask

**chews**
sweets, lollies

**chiack, shiack**
to tease; to throw off at

**chocker**
completely full

**chook**
a fowl or chicken; *to act like a headless chook*, to behave hysterically

**chuck a wobblie**
to have a fit of hysteria or faintness

**chuddy, chutty**
chewing-gum

**chunder**
(to) vomit

**clobbering machine**
a fanciful name for the Kiwi habit of cutting outstanding people down to size; a reaper of tall poppies

**cob(ber)**
a mate, especially as 'Me old cob'

**cobbler**
shearers' slang for the last (and usually the hardest to shear) sheep in a shearing pen

**cockabully**
a small freshwater fish (from Maori *kokopu(ru)*)

**cockie**
a farmer (formerly and usually on a small-holding); also *cow-cockie*, a dairy farmer; *sheep-cockie*, a pastoral farmer

**cockie's joy**
golden syrup or treacle

**coconut**
an offensive word for a Pacific Islander

**come a thud**
to fail in an enterprise

**cookshop**
the cookhouse of a workman's camp

**corker**
fine, beaut

**corporation**
a protruding stomach

**cot-case**
a person confined to bed through illness or injury

**cow-spanker**
a dairy-farmer

**crack a fat**
to achieve an erection

**crawler**
a toady, a sycophant; also as *crawlie*, a freshwater crayfish

**cray**
a crayfish, now called 'rock lobster'

**crib**
a southern South Island name for a holiday cottage, a bach; also, among miners and tunnellers, a meal break, a cut-lunch eaten at work

**crim**
a criminal

**crook**
ill; awry or broken; angry: as *feel crook*, ill; *go crook (at)*, to scold; *put one in crook with* (a boss, etc.), to put someone in ill favour with

**crookie**
an imperfect person or thing

**crow**
a workman on a haystack or grainstack who forks sheaves up for the stacker

**a crust**
a living: 'What do you do for a crust?'

**bit on the cuff**
a bit tough, rough, or unfair

**cunning as a shithouse rat**
very cunning

**cut**
finished, 'the keg's cut'; drunk, 'Mum's cut and the tea's ruined.'

**go like a cut cat**
to proceed at pace (a piquant
variant of *scalded cat*)

**cut the rough**
stop acting roughly or uncouthly,
'get off my back', ease off

**the cuts**
corporal punishment in school: 'I
got the cut's for leaving out
apostrophe's.'

**cuz(zy), cuzzy-bro**
a term of address or reference
used mainly among young Maori

# D

**dag**
an amusing character; a wag

**Dally**
a familiar, partially derogatory
form of 'Dalmatian', a New
Zealander of mainly Croatian
extraction

**daylight robbery**
said of exorbitant prices or
gouging (e.g. bank) charges

**work off a dead horse**
an old-fashioned expression for working off a debt (or an advance on wages)

**deadhouse**
an old gumfields' term for a hotel shed where drunks were put to sleep off their excesses

**deadman's arm**
steamed currant roll as a dessert (a poorman's *pavlova*)

**deal to (a person)**
to beat up, to thrash

**de facto**
of an interpersonal relationship, equivalent to legal marriage; a partner in such a relationship

**deli**
a delicatessen

**the demons, the dees**
detectives

**dero**
a human derelict

**dickhead**
a fool

**dig, Old Dig**
a (returned) serviceman; also used as a term of address

**dill**
a fool or stupid person

**ding**
a small dent in a car (originally in a surf-board)

**dingbats**
crazy; *in the dingbats*, in a fit of delirium tremens

**dinkum**
true, genuine, proper; *the dinkum oil*, correct information

**dinky-die**
truly, certainly: 'I *did* see a ghost, dinky-die!'

**dip out (on)**
to miss out (on)

**dirty Turk**
rhyming slang for 'work'

**dob in**
the kiwi game of reporting the peccadilloes of one's friends and neighbours to the authorities

**doctor**
a sheep-station or camp cook (originally a sea-cook)

**go for the doctor**
to risk all on a main chance

**turn dog on**
to go bad on, to turn sour on

**dogbox**
as *in the dogbox*, in bad odour
(with); in a place or attitude of
penance

**dole bludger**
an offensive name for those on
State support, especially those on
family or unemployment benefits

**doolan**
a Catholic

**dong**
to hit or strike: 'I'll dong ya if ya
don't stop howling.'

**donk**
a racehorse: 'I did my dough on
the donks.'

**donko**
the 'smoko' room of a workplace

**do one's block, bun, scone**
to lose control of one's
emotional self

**do one's dough**
to lose (or spend) all one's money

**do over**
to beat up, to 'work over': 'He was done over and his money stolen.'

**have a down on**
to have a grudge against

**down the gurgler**
of plans, etc., failed completely

**down to the wire**
of a contest, etc., excruciatingly closely contested

**drag the chain**
to lag behind one's fellows; not to 'tow the line'

**drongo**
a stupid fool

**drop one's bundle**
to fart; to defecate; to become upset, e.g. at others' bundle-dropping

**droppie**
a drop kick at rugby football: 'The winning points came when Gouger got a wee droppie over the bar.'

HIC!

**duff**
to make (a person)
pregnant

**up the duff**
pregnant

**drunk as a wheelbarrow**
unable to move without help

**duckshove**
to duck responsibility:
'Bureaucrats are born to
duckshove.'

**dunny**
a privy

**dyke**
a (usually outdoor) privy, a
long-drop

# E

**earbash**
to talk incessantly

**earbasher**
a person who steals the conversation from others

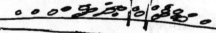

**take an early shower**
of a rugby player, to be sent off
the field for foul play

**eggshell blond**
a too-bald man

**ehoa**
mate, friend

**electric puha**
marijuana, or smoking greens
(*puha* Maori for 'sowthistle', a
popular pot herb)

**ewesterer**
a cross between a
ewe and a
musterer

# F

**fair cow**
of a person, thing or situation,
abominable

**fart sack**
a polite term for a sleeping-bag,
or bed

**financial**
having cash money

**fit as a buck rat**
very fit

**fizz or fizzy drink**
soft-drink, 'lolly water'

**fizz-boat**
a small powerboat

**flicks**
movies, pictures

**flog**
to steal

**fly cemetery**
a fruit square, comprising dried
fruit between two pastry layers

**flyblown**
broke, unfinancial

**footie**
rugby union or league

**full as a bull**
very drunk

**full as a tick**
ditto

# G

**gate**
mouth: 'Shut ya gate!'

**Gentle Annie**
a steep incline or hill
(*'Twas sweet upon a Summer's eve*
*To wander with my Nannie*
*To hop across the Roaring Meg*
*And climb up Gentle Annie.*
— C.E. Douglas, explorer, 1891)

**gerry**
a geriatric, anyone over thirty

**get stuck into**
to attack vigorously (a person, a
problem, a piece of work)

**get the willies**
be overcome with trepidation

**get your a into g**
(arse into gear) Hurry up!

**the GG**
the Governor-General (See *gyver* below.)

**gib-board**
gibraltar board, a proprietary 'gypsum' board

**gidday, g'die**
a commonly mumbled greeting

**gink**
a bloke; a look: 'Gis a gink at the photo.'

**give a car a haircut**
to rewind the speedo before a sale

**give it a burl**
give it a try

**go butchers (hook) at**
rhyming slang for *go crook at*, to go off at

**Godzone**
New Zealand as a post-Christian democracy. ('God's own country but the devil's own mess.' — Richard John Seddon, one-time Premier.)

**go for the doctor**
make a supreme effort

**go off pop at**
to scold

**from go to whoa**
from start to finish

**she's a gold watch**
everything's OK, 'good as gold'

**goob**
a gob of phlegm, especially as ejected by sportspeople in the public eye

**good on you**
said to encourage

**good-oh, goodo**
a term of agreement; OK, in fine style: 'She's getting along goodo.'

**goog, googie**
an egg: 'Who killed the goose that laid the golden googies?'

**goorie**
a mongrel dog (from Maori *kuri*, dog)

**graunch**
to grind noisily, as of metal scraping a rough surface

**graft**
(hard) work

**grafter**
a toiler: 'Some politicians are known as hard grafters.'

**greaser**
a fall (*to come a greaser*)

**greasies**
takeaways, especially fish and chips

WHOOPS!

**as greasy as a butcher's apron,
as greasy as a butcher's pup**
very greasy: 'The road was as greasy as a butcher's apron.'

**green cart**
the vehicle supposed to take one off to the lunatic asylum

**greenie**
a conservationist

**grog**
liquor of any kind, as in the gay rugby saying, 'No amount of grog will make a loose forward tight'.

**grot**
a toilet

**grouse**
fine, excellent

**gumbootette**
sounds like a rubber-shod marching girl, but really a small gumboot

**gumdigger**
dentist

**gummies**
gumboots (British 'wellies')

**gunga**
anus: 'You'll get a boot up the gunga if ya don't moderate your language!'

**gutser**
a heavy fall: 'Mum asked me if I'd come a gutser off my bike.'

**gutsful**
an ample sufficiency: 'I've had a gutsful of your bellyaching.'

**the gyver**
airs, side: 'They put on the gyver and a clean tablecloth when the GG came for a meal.'

# H

**run like a hairy goat**
to move at speed; of an engine, to
run roughly

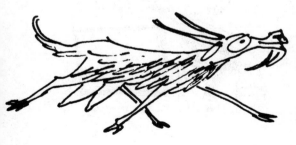

**half-gee**
a half-gallon flagon (of beer)

**half-pie**
incomplete, or incompletely:
'It was only half-pie finished off.'

**to have someone on one's
hammer**
to have someone on one's back:
'They've been on my hammer to
pay off my debts.'

**handle**
a 'pint' glass beer mug or its
contents

**hangman**
a hard-case or hard drinker; a
devil-may-care person: 'If you
give her enough rope you'll find
she's a bit of a hangman.'

**happy as a flea on a dog**
very happy

**happy as Larry**
ditto

I just like hangin' out
in the pub!!

**hard case**
an amusing or independent person; a rough diamond; a *dag*

**hard-hitter, hard-knocker**
old names for a bowler hat

**hard yacker**
hard work

**hash-foundry**
a restaurant or eating-house

**have gorse in one's pocket**
to be slow in paying one's share

**head sherang**
the big chief

**give it heaps**
give (something) a supreme effort

**the Hill**
Mt Eden prison, Auckland; Parliament Buildings, Wellington

**hoha**
fed up, tired; tiresome (from Maori *hoha*, wearied)

**holding**
having cash money

**hollywood**
a faked or exaggerated injury to gain a rest or advantage on a sports field

**home and dried,**
**home and hosed**
successful; safe and sound: 'Make
40 in the first innings and you'll
be home and hosed.'

**home on the pig's back**
successful, well-off

**hooer**
a term of mild abuse: from a
dialect pronunciation of 'whore'

**hook one's mutton**
to make off; also (formerly) to
take one's partner for a dance

**hoon**
a lout; as a verb, *to hoon around*, to
indulge in loutish behaviour

**hooped**
drunk: 'He rolled out the barrel and arrived home hooped.'

**hooray**
a Kiwi farewell

**hophead**
a heavy drinker

**the hops**
the downfall of the *hophead*

**hori**
an offensive word for a Maori

**House of Parliament**
a nickname for a privy

**'How would you be?'**
a greeting, 'How are you?'

**huckery**
(physically) unpleasant: 'That's a huckery-looking bloke.'

**humdinger**
excellent, beaut; or something excellent of its kind; formerly said to be the bell that hung on the back of a nightcart

# I

**illegal Tegel**
wild pigeon as food: pigeon is a
protected species, 'Tegel' is the
name of a popular brand of
frozen chicken

**in boots and all**
said of a vicious attack or a
vigorous rugby ruck

**Irish curtains**
cobwebs

# J

**jerry to**
to catch on, to understand:
'I didn't jerry to the fact they
were taking the mickey.'

**jigger**
a railways velocipede: 'The
stationmaster went to market and
brought a fat pig home by jigger.'

**Joe Blakes**
rhyming slang for 'shakes'

**Joe (Hunt)**
a fool

**john hop**
rhyming slang for 'cop'. From
original John (Dunn), a play on
'gendarme'

**joker**
a bloke: 'A good Kiwi joker is
seldom amusing.'

# K

**kai kart**
a pie cart often specialising in
Maori foods such as pies, seafood
and chips

**kapai**
good; often as an exclamation:
from Maori

**kero**
kerosene, often elsewhere called
paraffin

**kia ora**
Good luck! A Maori greeting now
used widely by non-Maori as a
mode of bicultural display

**kick up bobsidie**
to make a great fuss or noise

**kindy**
kindergarten

**king hit**
a knock-out punch

**kiwi**
a flightless bird; a New Zealand
person; a rugby league national
representative

**knockback**
a refusal

**knockdown**
an introduction to someone, not
necessarily a boxer

**on the knocker**
promptly: 'Their bills were
always paid on the knocker.'

**knock up**
to rouse, especially from sleep:
'I'll knock you up first thing in
the morning.'

**knuckle sandwich**
a fist in the teeth

# L

BAA!!

HUMBUG

**ladies a plate (or basket)**
bring a contribution of food

**lagerphone**
a refined tambourine made
of bottletops loosely nailed
to a broomstick, a musical
memorial to Kiwi ingenuity
and taste

**lamburger**
a sheep-meat hamburger

**Land of the Wrong White Crowd**
Aotoheroa-New Zealand

**land-shark**
a land speculator, a former name for a present curse

**larrikin**
a mischievous youth; a young hoodlum

**have a lash at**
to have a try at; to attempt: 'He had a lash at teaching, but was too bright for the job.'

**laughing gear**
the teeth

**to be away laughing**
to be successful, or well on the way to success

**lawyer**
a horrid thorny vine or bushy tangle from whose clutches a victim escapes with difficulty and at great personal cost

**leftfooter**
a Catholic

**lemon squeezer**
a felt hat, peaked and brimmed, and shaped like an old-fashioned lemon-squeezer; once regularly worn by New Zealand soldiers, now only as a ceremonial head-gear

**do a line with**
to make up to (a prospective love-object): 'And all the time she was doing a line with a bloke from Telecom.'

**littlie**
an infant child

**live on birdseed, live on the smell of an oily rag**
to live as a beneficiary or an anorexic

**log of wood**
a nickname for the Ranfurly Shield, a national rugby trophy

**lolly**
a sweet; *the lolly*, money; *lolly scramble*, the playful scattering of lollies (sweets) for children to scramble for; also, the opening of an election-year pork-barrel; *lolly water*, soft drink

The even longer drop.

**long acre**
the grazing along the side of a public road

**long drop**
an outdoor privy

**long john**
an oblong bread-loaf

**loopie**
a tourist

**loosie**
a loose rugby union forward, *not* a hooker (see also *grog* above)

**lux**
to use a vacuum cleaner, from the proprietary name 'Electrolux': 'I luxed the flat after the party.'

Just hangin' *loose*!

# M

**mad as a meat-axe**
very angry or crazy

**go maggoty**
to become angry: 'She went maggoty at the butcher, and went butchers at the baker.'

**Mainland**
the Big (or South) Island: 'I caught an interisland fairy for the Mainland.'

**make a sale**
to vomit

**makings**
tobacco and a tissue paper for *roll-your-owns*

**go to market**
to become angry: 'Gee, did he go to market when his neighbour called him a fat pig.'

**matagouri mermaid**
a legendary outback creature, the
virgin bride of a *wild Irishman*

**mate**
a familiar; also used as a term of
address to strangers

**mates rates**
reduced preferential rates for
friends and fellow-tradesmen
(*Musa Pedestris*, John S. Farmer's
anthology of slang rhymes
(1536–1896) quotes a 1660 ballad
possibly written by an emergent
Kiwi:
*We Bill all our Mates
   at very low rates,
While some keep their Quarters
   as high as the fates.*)

**message**
a shopping errand (e.g. to run messages)

**micky doolan**
a Catholic

**milkshake**
baking soda fed illicitly to race-horses as an aid to performance

**mingie**
*m*ean + st*ingy*: 'Only a dollar — ya mingie cow!'

**miserable as a shag**
very miserable

**mobster**
a member of the Mongrel Mob gang

**moke**
a (usually inferior) racehorse

C'MON MOKE!

**molly-dooker**
a left-handed person

**Mong(rel)**
same as *mobster*

**monte**
a certainty: 'Sudden Death's a monte to win the last race.'

**mountain oyster**
sheep's testicle eaten raw or fricasseed by local eunuchs

**muldoonery**
the policies (especially economic) and abrasive personal style of a former Prime Minister, the late R.D. Muldoon

**murder house**
a school dental clinic (according to children)

**my oath!**
indicating agreement or mild enthusiasm

**mystery bag**
a sausage or saveloy

# N

**nailrod**
an old name for a cheap, dark tobacco

**nark**
an irritating person

**narked**
annoyed

**Nat**
a National Party member: 'He was the biggest little Nat south of Palmerston North.'

**naughty**
a coy Kiwism for a bout of sexual intercourse

**neat**
a universal word of approval shared by New Zealand young

**game as Ned Kelly**
very plucky (Ned Kelly was the original 19th-century Australian bush entrepreneur)

**new chum**
one new to a job; (formerly) a newly-arrived immigrant

**in the nick**
naked

**the night's a pup**
'It's early yet.'

**ning-nong**
a failed no-hoper

**nippon-clipon**
a name for the Japanese-made extensions to the Auckland Harbour Bridge

**put the nips in**
to put pressure on

**no beg pardons**
said of a vigorous attack

**no fear!**
indicating refusal or disagreement

**no flies on**
said of a smart or shrewd person:
often, to a freckled person, tagged
'but you can see where they've
been'

**no good to Gundy**
an old-fashioned term for an
unfortunate or useless thing or
person

**no hoper**
a confirmed failure

**nobbler**
an old word for a glass or 'nip' of
spirits.

**nong**
a silly fool: 'The poor little nong
thinks deer velvet makes you
sexy.'

**North Cape to the Bluff**
from one end of New Zealand to
the other

**not much chop**
not very useful or advantageous

**not the full quid**
mentally deficient, not 'all there'

**not to have a (brass) razoo**
to be broke

**not to know one's arse from one's elbow**
to be thoroughly confused or ignorant

**not to know someone from a bar of soap**
not to recognise

**not to know whether one is Arthur or Martha**
to be totally confused or stupid

**not worth a tin of fish**
of little worth

**in the nuddy**
naked

I STILL CAN'T TELL THE DIFFERENCE!

# O

**OE, overseas experience**
the fledgling Kiwi's mandatory
trip to Europe

**off they go says Bob Munro**
a rhyming tag associated with
starting races or losing
appendages, etc.

**offsider**
the assistant of another, especially
of a cook

OFF THEY GO
SAYS BOB
MUNRO!

**get offside with a person**
to put oneself in wrong with someone: 'Jeez, did I get offside with the teacher.'

**old identity**
one who has lived long in one place; often an 'old nonentity'

**oldie**
a parent, or other aged person, especially one able to wield grey power

**on it**
on the booze

**on one's pat (malone)**
rhyming slang for 'on one's own'

**on the box seat**
in a situation of advantage

**on the never-never**
on time payment

**one out of the box**
said of anything fine or outstanding, especially of a fine day

**open slather**
a free-for-all

**ordinary bloke, ordinary joker, real Kiwi bloke**
the New Zealander, self-regarded as a touchstone of modesty and commonsense

**Oscar**
cash (old-fashioned rhyming slang, from the name *Oscar Asche*, an actor)

**Ossie**
Australia; (an) Australian

**out the monk**
unconscious; disabled

# P

**Parrie**
a familiar name for Paremoremo,
a strict boarding institution for
local élite

**pavlova, pav**
a New Zealand meringue
pudding with a fruit and cream
filling used as a dessert tease for
weight-watchers

**pea, pie, pud**
a traditional New Zealand *pie cart* meal (Rhymes with and often tastes like 'mud'.)

**perve**
to stare or ponder lustfully

**peter**
a till or cash-register; also a beer-flagon

**picnic**
a bothersome experience: 'There was an earthquake during the hui. What a picnic!'

**the pictures**
the cinema, the *flicks*

**pie cart**
a mobile cart selling meals and takeaway foods

**pie-on**
an old-fashioned word for fine, ship-shape: 'Grandma's kitchen was always pie-on.' (Maori *pai ana*.)

**Pig Islander**
a New Zealander

**Pig Islands**
New Zealand, from the number of resident swine

**piker**
one who fails in obligations; a coward

**a piece of piss**
something easily accomplished

**pisshead**
a heavy drinker

**plant**
to hide (something): 'She planted her ill-gotten gains up the manhole.'

**plastic fantastic**
a New Zealand name for a loser in a yacht race; also a credit card

**play-lunch**
a mid-morning snack taken by schoolchildren and consultants

**plonk**
liquor, especially cheap wine

**plutie**
moneyed, well-to-do (from *pluto*cratic)

**poke**
a twisted paper spill (or bag) — usually for lollies, occasionally for drugs

**poke the borax (or borak)**
to chaff or tease

I'll never drink again!

**poked**
exhausted: 'After a gay night on the town he woke up well and truly poked.'

**pole**
to steal

**pollie**
a politician

**Poly or Polly**
a Polynesian

**pom(mie)**
a Britisher, formerly 'homie'

**Pongolia**
Mother England

**poofter**
in old-fashioned speech, a skite or blowhard

**poor cow**
an unfortunate or miserable person

**possie, pozzie**
a position, a place of advantage

**poozle**
to scavenge for collectables:
'We spent our time poozling
under old houses.'

**pressie**
a present

**prez**
president, especially a gang
president

**puckeroo**
to break, ruin: from Maori
*pakaru*, broken

**puku**
stomach: from Maori *puku*,
stomach

Putting the boot
in the puku

OOF

**pull a fastie**
to put across a clever, usually
dishonest, stroke

**pull a swiftie**
ditto

**purge**
alcoholic liquor

**purler**
(1) a fall: 'He came a proper purler down the pub steps.'
(2) something fine or exceptional: 'We had a purler day scavenging at the local tip.'

**put one's pot on**
to report to the authorities, to *dob in*

**put the boot in**
to punish severely, especially an opponent who is down or weak

THE MORNING AFTER!

I feel purged!

# Q

**quack**
a medical doctor

**Queen Street farmer**
a businessman owning rural
property: from the name of
Auckland's main street

# R

**rabbit-killer**
a blow to the back of the neck
with the side of the hand

**rafferty('s) rules**
no rules at all

**rapt**
extremely pleased

**rare as rockinghorse shit**
very rare

**to have a rat**
to be eccentric or slightly crazy:
to be eccentrically singleminded
about something: 'She has a rat

about Aussies taking over
New Zealand.'

**ratbag**
an untrustworthy person, a
rogue

**rat house**
a psychiatric hospital

**rattle one's dags**
to hurry up: from the noise
of dry dags rattling as sheep
are driven along

**repo man**
a repossession agent

**rigger**
a beer-flagon

RATTLE YOUR DAGS!
THE REPO MAN'S
COMING.

OI!

REPO
ORDER

**ring-bolt**
to travel illicitly in a ship, hidden
in the crews' quarters

**ringer**
an expert

**a ring-in**
a substitute: 'You didn't tell me the ring-in's an All Black.'

**You can put a ring around that**
'That's for sure!'

**rip, shit, or bust**
a phrase indicating determination to finish a project regardless of the result

**Rogernomics**
an economic miracle played on an unsuspecting public

**roll-your-own**
a hand-rolled cigarette

**root**
to enforce sexual intercourse

**ropeable**
very angry

**rough as guts**
roughly made or turned out; uncouth

**rouseabout**
one who does various kinds of unskilled manual work

**rubberty-dub, rub-a-dub, rubbity**
rhyming slang for 'pub'

**rumpty dooler**
usually anything fine or superior:
'They say Katherine Mansfield
was a rumpty dooler on the
lagerphone; but I for one don't
believe it.'

**rustbucket**
a decrepit motor vehicle

# S

**scarce as hen's teeth**
very scarce

**scratcher**
a makeshift bed or sleeping bag

**scratchie**
a lottery ticket from which one scratches off a covering to reveal the prize

**scroggin**
a tramper's high-energy food of mixed dried fruit, nuts, etc.

**scunge**
a nasty, dirty, greasy person; hence *scungy* applied to such people and things

**sell out**
to vomit: 'He sold out in the family peonies.'

**send her down Hughie!**
an invocation to rain: Hughie is the highly effable name of a local *Jupiter Pluvialis*

**be sent down the road**
to be sacked

**septic tank**
rhyming slang for a 'bank': 'The septic tank's as safe as the Post Office clock.'

**session**
a drinking bout with acquaintances (kirk sessions are the exception)

**sexo**
a person oversexed but underpinned

**shake**
an earthquake

**s/he'd shit anywhere**
said of the socially adept personality easily able to fit in with any company

**she's or she'll be apples, jake, right**
it's all right, okay

**sheila**
a girl(friend); a woman

**shelf**
a police informer: 'Do the police
put old shelves out to grass?'

**shickered**
drunk: from Yiddish *shicker*,
drunk

**shimmy**
an old word for singlet
(*The boy stood on the burning deck
In nothing but his shimmy,
The flames rolled up, and up, and up,
And burned his little jimmy*.)

**ship-girl**
a prostitute working ships

**shivoo**
A party, a 'shindy' (from French *chez vous* 'at your place', the Kiwi's choice of venue)

**shonky**
dishonest, 'shady'; an anti-Semitic word much in vogue among political and financial commentators. (From *Shonky*, a Jew)

**shook on**
keen on, attracted to

**shoot through**
to leave suddenly

**shouse**
a familiar word for a lavatory: 'Quick, mate, show's ya shouse.'

**shout**
to treat; a treat, especially of liquor

**shrewdie**
a shrewd trick; a clever or tricky person

**shufti**
a look (at something)

**sickie**
a period of sick-leave from work, often caused by 'Mondayitis'

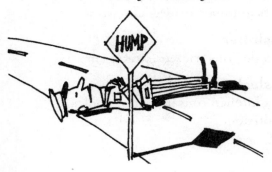

**silent policeman**
a raised strip across a road to control traffic speed

**silly as a two-bob watch, silly as a wet hen**
very silly

**sink the boot in**
to kick viciously, especially an opponent who is down

**sinker**
institutional steamed pudding

**sit up like jacky**
to sit up straight (and take notice); to sit up with obvious confidence

**six-o'clock closing**
a former method of insisting drunks go home for tea

**six-o'clock swill**
the *Pig Island* drinking scene when hotel bars were closed at six o'clock

**go for a skate**
to come a cropper: to take a fall

**skerrick**
a small piece, especially as 'not a skerrick left'

**skinner**
finished, empty: 'The food's a skinner.'

**skinnier than a gumdigger's dog**
very skinny

**skite**
to boast; boasting

**skull**
to sink beer quickly, especially in a drinking contest: from Scandinavian *skol*, a toast

**slinter**
a devious trick or stratagem

**slushy**
a kitchen rouseabout or cook's offsider

**smart-fart**
a feisty know-all ('Who blew you?' is the customary put-down. *Feisty* originally 'farty', from *fist* 'a fart', through United States figurative use for an excitable, aggressive small 'yap-dog'.)

**smoko, smoke-oh**
a refreshment break from work

**snaky**
of nasty or uncertain temper

**snarler**
sausage

**snitcher**
fine, excellent

**take a snitcher to**
to take a dislike to: 'He's liable to take a snitcher to door-knockers.'

**snivelling snufflebuster**
an old-fashioned name for a moaner or whinger

**snork**
a baby or young child

**sook(ie)**
a crybaby, a cowardly child; also a calf or a call to a calf

**all done up like a sore toe**
overdressed

**southerly buster**
a violent southerly gale

**to get a spark up**
to feel the exhilarating effects of
liquor: 'I drank five gallons the other night but couldn't get a spark up.'

**sparkie**
an electrician

**spieler**
a fast-talker; a con-man

**sport**
a form of address; 'mate': 'Howya sport?' 'Boxabirds.'

**spot**
a glass of liquor: 'Have another spot, m'dear.'

**spottie**
usually a small wrasse much fished by children from wharves and jetties

**sprig**
to rake a prone rugby opponent
with boot 'sprigs' (studs)

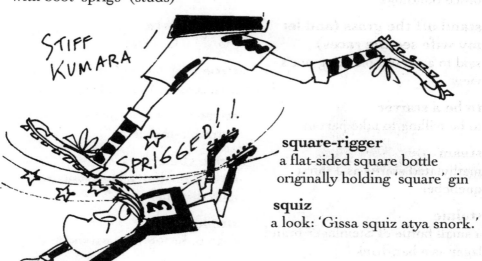

**square-rigger**
a flat-sided square bottle
originally holding 'square' gin

**squiz**
a look: 'Gissa squiz atya snork.'

**stair-dancer**
a thief whose beat is multi-storey office buildings

**stand off the grass (and let my wife see the races)**
said to a person blocking one's view

**to be a starter**
to be willing to take part in

**steam**
methylated spirits as a thirst quencher

**steinie**
a small bottle of Steinlager brand lager as a bar drink

**stickybeak**
an inquisitive person; to behave in an inquisitive way

**stiff kumara**
Hard luck, mate!

**stipe**
a racecourse (stipendiary) steward

**stirrer**
a trouble-maker

**stone the crows**
an exclamation of surprise or mild disbelief

**stonkered**
beaten, brought to a standstill

**stoush**
a fight, a brawl; brawling

**the strength of, the strong of**
the facts of, the *dinkum oil*:
'What's the strong of the story
that...'

**like a stunned mullet**
dazed: 'After the blow, he
wandered around like a stunned
mullet.'

**to suck the kumara**
to fail or lose out

**swiftie**
a shrewd or dishonest trick or
gambit

stunning!

# T

**taihoa**
'Wait on!'

**tall poppy**
an outstanding person ripe for
cutting down by inferiors or by
the Kiwi clobbering machine

**tangi**
a party; from *tangi*, a Maori
funeral ceremony

**Taranaki gate**
a makeshift gate of wire and
battens

**tart**
a woman, seldom loose

**tasty**
of cheese, more mature than
'soapy'

**tatt**
a tattoo, especially (as *boob tatt*)
an amateur tattoo on face or
hands to mark a stay in prison

**technicolour yawn**
a vari-coloured vomiting

**the Other Side**
Australia

**thick as pigshit**
of a person, exceedingly brainless

**Think Big**
a name given to public policies
and works whose cost exceeds
their uselessness

**tickle the peter**
regularly to take money from the
till

**tight as a duck's arse (and
that's watertight)**
said of a person mean with money

**till the cows come home**
indicating a longish period with
no promise of success at the end
of it: 'You can cry till the cows
come home, but you're not
watching the late programme.'

**tinny**
lucky

**tinpot**
(often of a place) small, insignificant

**to chat someone**
to give corrective advice to, to put a person in the know

**toby**
the mains stopcock controlling water delivery to properties: from Scottish dialect

**toey**
excitable; on edge; fast off the mark

**tonky**
fashionable, trendy

**toot**
*tutu*, a plant whose leaves can poison stock

**top shelf**
spirits as a bar-drink: 'If it's your shout, I'll have top-shelf stuff.'

**toss the tiger**
to vomit

**toss one's lollies**
ditto (Both are variants of *technicolour yawn*, drawing attention to the variegated results of the exercise)

**towie**
a tow-truck driver

GROWLLLL!!!

**town bike**
a person free with sexual favours

**troppo**
crazy

**trots**
a race-meeting for trotting or
pacing horses

**tyre-kicker**
a politician who talks round but
evades difficult choices (like a
person who inspects but never
buys in a used-car yard)

# U

**underground mutton**
rabbit meat as food

**up the duff**
pregnant

**up you!**
an exclamation of dismissal

**up the wop**
awry; pregnant

**use a five-fingered chequebook**
to steal or shoplift

I SHOULD'VE USED A CONDOM!.

# V

**vegies**
vegetables

**violets**
a condition of great public
concern: 'Police are worried
about growing violets in
Auckland.'

# W

**waddy**
a club or heavy stick

**wake up to**
alert to: 'He was wake up to my tricks straightaway.'

**wear**
general English slang for 'tolerate': 'I won't wear the insolence of these colonials.'

**'Were you born in a tent?'**
said to a person leaving a door open

**whack into**
to attack (foes, work, food) vigorously

**wharfie**
a wharf labourer (docker; longshoreman)

**whips of**
plenty of: 'They had whips of money to spend.'

**whole shooting-box**
everything or everyone; the 'whole box of tricks'

**w(h)op-c(r)acker**
something outstanding of its kind; a great lie

**Whykickamookau**
an imaginary place, whose form parodies that of Maori place-names

**widgie**
a subcultural female of the 1950s

**wild Irishman**
matagouri, a thorny, difficult plant of open country

**windie**
a (Caribbean) wind-surfer

**within coo-ee of**
within reach of; *not to come within coo-ee of*, to come nowhere near a goal

**throw a wobbly**
to have a fit of temper or high emotion: 'Children have tantrums; adults throw wobblies.'

**woop-woops, wop-wops**
usually *up* or *in the wop-wops*, the remote areas

**wouldn't it!**
expressing surprise, exasperation: 'Wouldn't it rock ya, eh?'

**wowser**
a puritanical spoilsport; one who disapproves of pleasures other than her or his own

# Y

**yahoo**
to act the lout in a noisy fashion

**you can put a ring round that**
indicating a strong affirmative
emphasis

# Z

**zambuck**
a first-aid person of the Order of
St John, especially when
attending a sports gathering: from
the name of a once-popular brand
of ointment, 'Zam-buk'

**ziff**
an old-fashioned word for a
beard: 'A patriarchal ziff hid his
true feelings for grandma.'